First published in Great Britain in 2005 by:

AFN Publishing Ltd
PO Box 1558
Gerrards Cross
Buckinghamshire
SL9 0XL

www.afnpublishing.co.uk

ISBN 0-9538487-2-8

ELEVEN PLUS

VERBAL REASONING TECHNIQUES
&
PRACTICE QUESTIONS

A F N
Publishing

AFN Publishing Ltd

www.afnpublishing.co.uk

Guidance Notes

The objective of this book is to familiarise children with the types of questions found on eleven plus and twelve plus secondary selection tests and to explain the techniques for answering them. It can be used to prepare for multiple-choice versions of the selection tests as well as traditional format tests.

The book provides example questions and step-by-step approaches that explain the techniques for answering questions. It also contains practice questions for common question types and gives useful hints and tips to save time and avoid mistakes.

It is important that your child's confidence and abilities are developed whilst working through this book and the following approach is recommended.

Step 1

Read through the instructions contained in the example question with your child and check that they fully understand what the question is asking them to do. Encourage them to start thinking about how they might approach the problem.

Once your child understands what the question is asking for, allow them to look at the example question so they are aware of the format and have the opportunity to clarify anything that they are unsure of.

Step 2

Work through the suggested technique with your child, one step at a time. Apply the technique to the example and ensure that your child understands the process that they will need to follow when answering the practice questions.

Step 3

Go through the "Hints & Tips" with your child. These can significantly help to reduce the time taken to answer questions and can help to avoid common errors. They can also help to build confidence.

Step 4

Work through the first example question with your child by applying the recommended technique.

You should then allow your child to work through the other practice questions alone but should ensure that you are available to answer queries, or provide clarification, when needed.

Step 5

Finally, mark the practice questions with your child and work through any errors together.

Further Practice

If your child needs further practise after completing the practice questions in this book, you may find the following Eleven Plus Verbal Reasoning Practice Tests useful:

Multiple-Choice Eleven Plus Verbal Reasoning Papers 1 to 4	ISBN 0-9538487-1-X
Multiple-Choice Eleven Plus Verbal Reasoning Papers 5 to 8	ISBN 0-9538487-4-4
Traditional Format Eleven Plus Verbal Reasoning Papers 1 to 4	ISBN 0-9538487-3-6
Traditional Format Eleven Plus Verbal Reasoning Papers 5 to 8	ISBN 0-9538487-5-2

Details of these and other publications can be found at **www.afnpublishing.co.uk**

QUESTION TYPE 1 – "Letters and Numbers"

Example Question

In the following question, numbers have been replaced with letters. You need to work out the answer to the sum.

Example: If A = 6, B = 4, C = 2 and D = 1, find the answer to this sum and **write it as a number**.

A + B + D = [11]

Explanation and Technique

To answer this type of question you must first translate the formula from letters to numbers. The best way to do this is to work from left to right and write the numbers above or below the letters on the question paper. Once you have done this you can then calculate the answer.

In the example above if A equals 6, B equals 4, C equals 2 and D equals 1, then the formula:

A + B + D =

can be re-written as shown below by replacing the letters with numbers:

6 + 4 + 1 =

Once you have translated the values from letters to numbers you just need to work out the sum. In this example the answer to 6 + 4 + 1 is 11.

You should always check how the examiner wants you to provide your answer. In the example above you are asked to calculate your answer as a **number**. However you may be asked to provide your answer as a **letter**. If this is the case you must first calculate the answer as a number and then translate this into a letter using the key provided in the question.

Hints & Tips

Read the question carefully to check whether you need to give your answer as a **number** or a **letter**.

Re-check your calculation – it is very easy to make an arithmetic error.

Write the numbers above or below the letters on the question sheet rather than trying to remember them in your head. This will help you to avoid errors and help you to check your calculation.

Practice Questions

In the following questions numbers have been replaced with letters. You need to work out the answers to the sums. ***Example:*** If A = 5, B = 4, C = 3 and D = 2, find the answer to this sum and **write it as a number**. A + B + C = [**12**]	
1.1	If A = 5, B = 4, C = 3 and D = 2, find the answer to this sum and **write it as a number**. A - B + D = [ ]
1.2	If A = 1, B = 4, C = 10 and D = 15, find the answer to this sum and **write it as a letter**. D - A - B = [ ]
1.3	If A = 3, B = 6, C = 9 and D = 12, find the answer to this sum and **write it as a letter**. A x D ÷ B = [ ]
1.4	If A = 6, B = 4, C = 10 and D = 20, find the answer to this sum and **write it as a number**. A + B - C = [ ]
1.5	If A = 6, B = 7, C = 8 and D = 9, find the answer to this sum and **write it as a number**. A + B + C - D = [ ]
1.6	If A = 20, B = 15, C = 10 and D = 5, find the answer to this sum and **write it as a letter**. A - B + D = [ ]
1.7	If A = 1, B = 2, C = 4 and D = 8, find the answer to this sum and **write it as a number**. A x B x D x C = [ ]
1.8	If A = 2, B = 3, C = 4 and D = 5, find the answer to this sum and **write it as a letter**. D + C - A - B = [ ]

QUESTION TYPE 2 – "Double Trouble"

Example Question

In the question below there are two sets of words. Find a word that goes equally well with both sets.

Example: [clay, soil] [globe, world] [earth]

Explanation and Technique

In this question you are being asked to find one word that is related to the words in both sets of brackets. The word will have two different uses.

To answer these questions you should look for words that are associated with the words in the first set of brackets. As you think of a word check to see if this can be linked with the words in the second set of brackets. If you can't find a word using this approach, think about words that can be associated with the words in the second brackets and then check to see if these can be linked with the words in the first set of brackets.

In the example above the answer is earth which is another word for soil and clay and is also a word that can be used instead of globe or world.

Hints & Tips

If you are taking a multiple-choice version of the test you will be given a list of words and asked to select one. In this case it is easier to match these words against the words in the brackets, rather than trying to spend time thinking about all the alternative words that may be suitable.

Practice Questions

In the questions below there are two sets of words. Find a word that goes equally well with both sets.

Example: [chime, clang] [hoop, circle] [ring]

2.1	[destroy, smash]	[stop, cease]	[ ]
2.2	[release, liberate]	[costless, gratis]	[ ]
2.3	[thriving, healthy]	[waterhole, spring]	[ ]
2.4	[recline, rest]	[fabricate, fib]	[ ]

2.5	[outing, journey]	[fall, stumble]	[ ]
2.6	[attach, glue]	[baton, twig]	[ ]
2.7	[girder, joist]	[radiate, glow]	[ ]
2.8	[solemn, serious]	[tomb, crypt]	[ ]

QUESTION TYPE 3 – "Complete the Sentence"

Example Question

In this question find one word from each pair of brackets that will complete the sentence in the most sensible way.

Example: High is to [<u>low</u>, height, tall] as wet is to [water, sea, <u>dry</u>].

Explanation and Technique

In this type of question you need to look for the relationship of the words outside the brackets with the words inside the brackets. You must find the <u>same</u> relationship between both sets of words.

The best way to do this is to concentrate on the first set of words and identify how they are related. Once you have identified this you can check whether the same relationship exists in the second set of words.

In the example question, high is the <u>opposite</u> of low and wet is the <u>opposite</u> of dry so it is the most sensible option.

Hints & Tips

There are many ways in which words can be related but you may find the following checklist helpful:

- Words with opposite meanings (such as sad and happy).
- Words with similar meanings (such as fast and rapid).
- Words that are pronounced the same but spelt differently (such as no and know).
- Objects that go together (such as stamp and letter).
- Words with different tenses (such as fly and flew).

Practice Questions

In these questions find one word from each pair of brackets that will complete the sentence in the most sensible way. ***Example:*** Cub is to [scout, sheep, <u>fox</u>] as kitten is to [<u>cat</u>, dog, pet].	
3.1	London is to [city, England, Bristol] as Rome is to [Italy, Spain, France].
3.2	Cold is to [ice, hot, freeze] as first is to [last, win, fast].
3.3	Nose is to [knows, face, smell] as write is to [pencil, right, letter].
3.4	Astronaut is to [Moon, space, rocket] as sailor is to [ship, navy, sail].
3.5	Run is to [ran, running, marathon] as walk is to [legs, walked, jog].
3.6	Snowdrop is to [flower, snow, daisy] as elm is to [leaf, road, tree].
3.7	Old is to [pension, ancient, oldest] as lofty is to [high, short, wide].
3.8	Gaggle is to [goose, coat, work] as shoal is to [bird, snake, fish].

QUESTION TYPE 4 – "Hidden Words"

Example Question

In the sentence below you must find a four-letter word that is hidden at the end of one word and the start of the next word. You must not change the order of the letters.

Example: The prie<u>st ar</u>rived at the church.

Explanation and Technique

To answer this type of question you need to find a **four-letter** word that starts at the end of one word and finishes at the beginning of the next word. Remember that you are not allowed to change the order of the letters.

The best way to do this is to work <u>methodically</u> from left to right. Start by looking at the last three letters of the first word and the first letter of the second word. If this doesn't make a word, move on to the last two letters of the first word and first two letters of the second word. If you don't find the word see if you can identify the word using the last letter of the first word and the first three letters of the second word.

If you don't find the hidden word between the first and second word, try the same approach to find a word between the second and third words. Continue with this approach, moving from left to right until you find the word.

Hints & Tips

Only look for four-letter words.

Remember that you only need to look at the **last three and first three** letters of consecutive words. Don't waste time looking at any other letters.

You will become better at answering this type of question with practise. You can practise the technique using any book or magazine and trying to find words hidden between other words.

You may find it useful to imagine that you have a "window" that you can move from left to right that will only allow you to see four letters at a time.

Practice Questions

In the sentences below you must find a four-letter word that is hidden at the end of one word and the start of the next word. You must not change the order of the letters.

Example: The rabbit enjoys lettuce and carrots.

4.1	The child entered the classroom cautiously.
4.2	Water makes the plants grow quickly.
4.3	The boys and girls worked diligently.
4.4	They thought that she would win.
4.5	The computer never really works properly.
4.6	When should I do my homework?
4.7	The girl asked to borrow something.
4.8	Did a chicken cross the road?

QUESTION TYPE 5 – "Similar Meanings"

Example Question

In the question below find **two** words, one from each group, that are **similar** in meaning.

Example: [wise, want, ancient] [clever, row, establish]

Explanation and Technique

The best way to answer this type of question is to start by looking at the first word in the left-hand brackets and compare this to all the words in the right-hand bracket to see if they are similar in meaning.

If you don't find a word with a similar meaning then move on and compare the second word in the left-hand brackets with the three words in the right-hand brackets.

If you still haven't found two words that are similar then compare the last word in the left-hand brackets with those in the right-hand brackets.

Hints & Tips

Read the question carefully! In some questions you may be asked to find two words that are **opposite** in meaning (such as new and old).

Always work systematically from left to right - that way you won't miss anything.

Do not waste time looking for other alternatives. As soon as you find two words that are similar in meaning, go on to the next question.

Practice Questions

In the questions below find **two** words, one from each group, that are **similar** in meaning.

Example: [press, stop, gather] [halt, loud, home]

5.1	[raise, jail, rodent]	[rusty, higher, defend]
5.2	[mobile, modern, glass]	[movable, test, spy]
5.3	[hobby, gone, rest]	[truth, bright, relax]
5.4	[empire, ale, pull]	[drag, soak, snuggle]

5.5	[sociable, refine, play]	[take, improve, trap]
5.6	[jest, wake, steady]	[joke, deafen, prize]
5.7	[waist, smudge, wail]	[velvet, wagon, cry]
5.8	[tidy, smear, warm]	[uphold, spread, quiet]

QUESTION TYPE 6 – "Letter Move"

Example Question

In the question below you must move one letter from the word on the left to the word on the right to make two new words. You are only allowed to move one letter and must not re-arrange any of the other letters.

Example: PEACH MALE [Each] [Maple]

Explanation and Technique

This question asks you to form **two** new words by transferring a **single letter** from the first word to the second word without re-arranging the order of any other letters. In the example shown, P has been moved from the word PEACH to form the words EACH and MAPLE.

To answer this type of question look at the first word and, working from left to right, remove one letter at a time until a new word is formed.

Try putting the letter that you have removed at the beginning of the second word to see if a new word is formed. If a new word is not formed put the letter between the first and second letters of the second word. Continue with this approach, working from left to right until you form another new word.

If you do not find a second new word go back to the first word and try removing different letters until a new word is formed. When you find another word, again insert the letter you have removed from the first word into the second word to see if a new word is formed. Continue with this process until you find **two** new words.

Hints & Tips

Work methodically from left to right. Using this approach will ensure that you do not miss any alternatives.

Practice Questions

In the questions below you must move one letter from the word on the left to the word on the right to make two new words. You are only allowed to move one letter and must not re-arrange any of the other letters.

Example: BOAT TALE [Oat] [Table]

6.1	FALL	EAR	[ ]	[ ]
6.2	HOUSE	FOND	[ ]	[ ]
6.3	CART	ROW	[ ]	[ ]
6.4	REACH	EAR	[ ]	[ ]
6.5	FOUR	MOTH	[ ]	[ ]
6.6	SCARF	ARM	[ ]	[ ]
6.7	TOWN	NEW	[ ]	[ ]
6.8	FOWL	EEL	[ ]	[ ]

QUESTION TYPE 7 – "Missing Letters"

Example Question

In the following question the underlined word has had three consecutive letters removed. These three letters make a word without being rearranged. What is the three-letter word?

Example: The ice was extremely <u>spery</u>. [lip]

Explanation and Technique

This type of question asks you to find a missing **three-letter** word that has been removed from another word in the sentence.

The sentence will usually give some clues about the word that has had letters removed so study it carefully. In the example above the sentence is about ice and the word that has had the letters removed is slippery. Remember that you do not need to re-arrange any of the letters.

Hints & Tips

If you are taking a multiple-choice test, look at the options on the answer sheet to see which may be suitable. This will save you time.

Only look for three letter words. Don't waste time looking for other words.

Do not spend too much time on any one question. It is very easy to spend too long looking for a word in this type of question. If you can't find the word quickly move on to the next question and return at the end of the exam, if you have time.

Practice Questions

In the following questions the underlined word has had three consecutive letters removed. These three letters make a word without being rearranged. What is the three-letter word?

Example: The soccer match will be held on urday. [Sat]

7.1	That dog ked loudly at the postman.	[ ]
7.2	The arc fired the arrow at the target.	[ ]
7.3	The builder pushed the wheelbar.	[ ]
7.4	She went running every day to train for the mahon.	[ ]
7.5	The eleph is the largest animal I have ever seen.	[ ]
7.6	The cher wrote the homework on the blackboard.	[ ]
7.7	The par repeated everything that the pirate said.	[ ]
7.8	The mon jumped from tree to tree.	[ ]

QUESTION TYPE 8 – "Missing Codes"

Example Question

There are four words and three code numbers written below. The codes are in a different order to the words and one code is missing.

Example: FOOD DEAL FILL DONE

7955 4283 4365

What is the code for DALE?

Explanation and Technique

In this example you need to find the code for DALE but you must first work out the number that corresponds to each letter by working logically. The best way to approach this is to study the words carefully and to identify where there are duplicate or unique letters. In the example above, the letter O appears twice in the word FOOD. In the example none of the codes have two numbers next to each other so the codes given do not relate to the word FOOD but must relate to the words DEAL, FILL and DONE.

The letters F and I in FILL do not appear in DEAL or DONE and so the code for FILL must be 7955 since 7 and 9 are unique. This can be confirmed since the first letters of DEAL and DONE are the same and must therefore be 4.

You also know that E is the last letter in the word DONE and the second letter in the word DEAL. Therefore the code for DEAL must be 4365 and the code for DONE must be 4283. You can now easily work out the code for FOOD and can record the codes and letters together as shown below:

7 2 2 4	4 3 6 5	7 9 5 5	4 2 8 3
FOOD	DEAL	FILL	DONE

Finding the code for the word DALE (or any other words) is now easy. You simply substitute the letters for numbers using the table above. The code for DALE is therefore 4653.

Hints & Tips

Take care! Make sure that you work out the codes carefully since if you get these wrong you will not be able to answer any of the questions in the section.

Write down your workings clearly – don't try and remember codes in your head since you will need to refer to these when you answer all the questions.

Practice Questions

There are four words and three code numbers written below. The codes are in a different order to the words and one code is missing. FORD CARE FEAR CARD 4857 4325 6257	
8.1	What is the code number for FOOD?
8.2	What is the code number for DARE?
8.3	Which word has the code number 48563?
8.4	What is the code number for FADE?
8.5	Which word has the code number 4253?
8.6	What is the code number for RACE?
8.7	Which word has the code number 7335?
8.8	Which word has the code number 4263?

QUESTION TYPE 9 – "Alphabet Search"

Example Question

In the following question the pairs of letters are related in the same way. Use the alphabet shown below to work out the missing letters.

A B C D E F G H I J K L M N O P Q R S T U V W X Y Z

Example: AB is related to CE as KL is related to [MO]

Explanation and Technique

In this question you must work out where letters in the alphabet are in relation to other letters. The technique is best explained using the example question.

AB is related to CE as KL is related to?

In these questions letters are presented in pairs, for example, AB or CE. However, to answer these questions you **must** treat the **first and second letter in each pair separately**.

Start with the first letters in the pairs and use the alphabet to work out how they are related. In the example, C is **two** letters to the **right** of A:

A B **C** D E F G H I J K L M N O P Q R S T U V W X Y Z

So the first letter in the answer will be **two** letters to the **right** of K, i.e. **M**.

A B **C** D E F G H I J **K** L **M** N O P Q R S T U V W X Y Z

Now look at the second letters in the pairs. E is **three** letters to the **right** of B. Using the same logic the letter that you are looking for will be **three** letters to the **right** of L, i.e. **O**.

A **B** C D **E** F G H I J K **L** M N **O** P Q R S T U V W X Y Z

Finally you need to combine the letters you have found. In the example, the answer is **MO**.

In the example you needed to count to the right from one word to another but in some questions it may be easier to count to the left.

Hints & Tips

Use the alphabet provided to work out how the letters are related – it is there to help you.

Always treat the first and second letters in the pairs **separately**.

Practice Questions

In the following questions the pairs of letters are related in the same way. Use the alphabet shown below to work out the missing letters.

A B C D E F G H I J K L M N O P Q R S T U V W X Y Z

Example: DX is related to EW as PG is related to [QF]

9.1	JX is related to GW as PG is related to	[ ]
9.2	LV is related to PQ as TR is related to	[ ]
9.3	VO is related to XQ as EI is related to	[ ]
9.4	AC is related to FA as RW is related to	[ ]
9.5	DD is related to JG as TP is related to	[ ]
9.6	HI is related to HA as YX is related to	[ ]
9.7	RQ is related to TT as JM is related to	[ ]
9.8	FO is related to CH as SP is related to	[ ]

QUESTION TYPE 10 – "Calculate the Number"

Example Question

In the following question calculate the number that will complete the sum.

Example: 9 + 3 = 14 - ? [2]

Explanation and Technique

These questions ask you to find a missing number that will complete the calculation. The best way to do this is by first working out the side of the equation where all the numbers are given.

In the example above, first calculate the sum on the left of the equals sign, i.e. 9 + 3 equals 12. Then use this number to find the missing number on the right of the equals sign. In this case the calculation becomes: 12 = 14 - ? Once you have done this you can easily work out that the answer is 2.

Hints & Tips

Try writing out the question once you have found the answer to one side of the equation. This can often make it easier and reduce the chance of making a mistake.

Practice Questions

In the following questions calculate the number that will complete each sum.

Example: 2 + 4 = 8 - ? [2]

10.1	8 + 7 = 3 + ?	[ ]
10.2	21 - 11 = 19 - ?	[ ]
10.3	18 x 4 = 3 x 10 + ?	[ ]
10.4	17 + 4 - 5 = 12 + 4 + ?	[ ]
10.5	21 ÷ 3 = 2 x 3 + ?	[ ]
10.6	120 ÷ 10 x 2 = ? + 20	[ ]
10.7	20 x 4 - 69 = 7 x 6 - ?	[ ]
10.8	144 ÷ 12 + 12 = ? x 3 x 4	[ ]

QUESTION TYPE 11 – "Two Groups"

Example Question

In this question there are two groups of words. The word in the left-hand brackets has been formed in a certain way using letters from the other words on the left-hand side. Use the letters in the words on the right-hand side to form a word **in the same way**.

Example: CORN [COME] MEAT : LOAF [LOSE] SEND

Explanation and Technique

In this type of question you need to identify how the word inside the brackets is formed using the two words outside the brackets.

In the example above, C in the word COME is the first letter in the word to the left of the **first** brackets i.e. **C**ORN. Therefore the first letter in the word that you need to find will be the first letter in the word to the left of the **second** brackets, i.e. **L**OAF. The relationship between the words is shown below:

CORN [COME] MEAT : LOAF [LOSE] SEND

The second letter in the word COME is O which is the second letter in the word to the left of the **first** brackets. Using the same logic, the second letter in the word that you need to find will be the second letter in the word to the left of the **second** brackets, i.e. L**O**AF:

CORN [COME] MEAT : LOAF [LOSE] SEND

The third letter in the word COME is M which is the first letter in the word MEAT which is found to the right of the **first** brackets. Therefore the third letter that you need to find will also be the first letter in the word to the right of the **second** brackets:

CORN [COME] MEAT : LOAF [LOSE] SEND

The final letter in the word COME is E which is the second letter in the word MEAT which is to the right of the **first** brackets. Therefore the word that you need to find will be the second letter in the word to the right of the **second** set of brackets, i.e. E.

CORN [COME] MEAT : LOAF [LOSE] SEND

Once you have found all the letters simply combine them to find the answer. In the example the answer is LOSE.

Hints & Tips

Always work carefully from left to right.

Write down the letters as you find them so that you don't forget them.

Practice Questions

In these questions there are two groups of words. The word in the left-hand brackets has been formed in a certain way using letters from the other words on the left-hand side. Use the letters in the words on the right-hand side to form a word **in the same way**.

Example: BATH [THIS] FIST : STAR [ARCH] ECHO

11.1	LAST [STOP] OPEN	:	CODE [ ] ARMS
11.2	FARM [SAFE] SELL	:	TARN [ ] LEAD
11.3	FOAL [LOAN] NEWT	:	CARD [ ] KISS
11.4	BOLD [BOAT] HATCH	:	RING [ ] SCENE
11.5	TEAL [MEET] SEAM	:	MAID [ ] TROT
11.6	CONE [HOME] MASH	:	FLOP [ ] ALES
11.7	BLOT [BAIT] RAID	:	PIER [ ] LOUD
11.8	ANGEL [LEAN] MOLE	:	ARISE [ ] HOPE

QUESTION TYPE 12 – "Number Sequences"

Example Question

In the question below find the number that continues the sequence.

Example: 10, 13, 16, 19, [22]

Explanation and Technique

In this type of question you are asked to identify the next number in a sequence so you must start by working from left to right to identify the sequence of the numbers that you are given.

In the example above each number in the sequence is 3 greater than the previous one. So the answer is 3 greater than 19, i.e. 22.

A good way to identify the sequence is to consider whether the numbers are increasing or decreasing. If the numbers are **increasing** then the next number in any given sequence will either be an **addition** to the previous number or a **multiplication** of it. If the numbers are **decreasing** then the next number in the sequence will be either a **subtraction** or a **division** of the previous number.

In some instances the differences between numbers in a sequence may not all be the same. In the following example the difference is increasing:

1, 2, 4, 7, 11,

The difference between 1 and 2 is 1, the difference between 2 and 4 is 2, the difference between 4 and 7 is 3, and the difference between 7 and 11 is 4. Each time the difference is increasing by 1. Therefore, as shown below, the next number in the sequence would be 11 plus 5, i.e.16.

1, 2, 4, 7, 11, **16**

+1 +2 +3 +4 +5

In some cases you may be given a sequence that is more complicated and trickier to solve. Look at the following sequence:

2, 8, 4, 9, 6, 10, 8,

At first glance the numbers do not appear to follow a logical sequence. In fact there are two sequences here. The first is 2, 4, 6, 8:

2, 8, 4, 9, 6, 10, 8,

and the second is 8, 9, 10:

2, 8, 4, 9, 6, 10, 8,

Therefore the next number in the sequence will be 11.

Hints & Tips

Remember that in some cases the difference between numbers may not always be the same.

Always start by identifying whether the numbers are increasing or decreasing.

If the sequence doesn't seem logical, check to see whether there is more than one sequence.

Practice Questions

In the questions below find the number that continues the sequence.

Example: 2, 4, 6, 8, [10]

12.1	6, 10, 14, 18,	[ ]
12.2	2, 4, 8, 16, 32,	[ ]
12.3	20, 17, 14, 11,	[ ]
12.4	256, 64, 16, 4,	[ ]
12.5	26, 21, 17, 14,	[ ]
12.6	2, 3, 5, 8, 12, 17,	[ ]
12.7	4, 3, 6, 6, 8, 9, 10,	[ ]
12.8	20, 8, 18, 9, 16, 10,	[ ]

QUESTION TYPE 13 – "Code Breakers"

Example Question

In the following question some of the words have been written in code. In the question the code has been "broken" for one word. You must use the same code to work out the second word.

The alphabet has been printed to help you.

A B C D E F G H I J K L M N O P Q R S T U V W X Y Z

Example: If SQVI means ROSE, what does IGOT mean? [HELP]

Explanation and Technique

For these questions you need to identify how the codes and words are related by using the alphabet provided. Look at the example question:

If SQVI means ROSE, what does IGOT mean?

In this question you are asked to find a word for the code IGOT **so use the first <u>code</u> as your starting point**. Start by looking at the **<u>first letter</u>** in the code **S**QVI and see how this relates to the **<u>first letter</u>** in the word **R**OSE.

A B C D E F G H I J K L M N O P Q R S T U V W X Y Z

You will see from the alphabet that R is **one letter to the left** of S. Using this same logic the first letter in the word that you are trying to find will be **<u>one letter to the left</u>** of I (the first letter in the code **I**GOT), i.e. H.

Now look at the **<u>second letter</u>** in the code S**Q**VI. O in the word R**O**SE is **<u>two letters to the left</u>** of Q so the second letter in the word that you are trying to find will also be **<u>two letters to the left</u>** of G (the second letter in the code word I**G**OT), i.e. E.

Now turn to the **<u>third letter</u>** in the code SQ**V**I. S in the word RO**S**E is **<u>three letters to the left</u>** of V so the third letter in the word that you are trying to find will also be **<u>three letters to the left</u>** of O (the third letter in the code word IG**O**T), i.e. L.

Finally look at the **<u>last letter</u>** in the code SQV**I**. E in the word ROS**E** is **<u>four letters to the left</u>** of I so the last letter in the word that you are trying to find will also be **<u>four letters to the left</u>** of T (the final letter in the code word IGO**T**), i.e. P.

Now all you need to do is to put together the letters you have found to form the word HELP.

In some questions you may be asked to work out a code for a word, as in the following example:

Example: If SFTU is the code for REST, what is the code for WISE?

It is important that you recognize that this question is asking for something different than the previous example. This time you need to work out the code for a word that you are given. The technique is slightly different since you **start by using the first <u>word</u> as your starting point** – in the example you start with the word REST.

Look at the first letter in the word **R**EST and see how the first letter in the code **S**FTU relates to this using the alphabet shown below.

A B C D E F G H I J K L M N O P Q R S T U V W X Y Z

As you will see, S is **<u>one letter to the right</u>** of R in the alphabet. Using the same logic, the first letter of the code that you are trying to find will also be **<u>one letter to the right</u>** of W (the first letter in the word **W**ISE), i.e. X.

Continue by looking at the second letter in the word R**E**ST. You will see that F in the code S**F**TU is one letter to the right of E in the alphabet. Therefore the code that you are trying to find will be one letter to the right of I (the second letter in the word WISE), i.e. J.

Now look at the third letter in the word REST. Using the alphabet, you will see that T in the code SFTU is one letter to the right of S. Therefore the code that you are trying to find will be one letter to the right of S (the third letter in the word WISE), i.e. T.

Finally look at the last letter in the word REST. You will see that U in the code SFTU is one letter to the right of T in the alphabet. Therefore the code that you are trying to find will be one letter to the right of E (the last letter in the word WISE), i.e. F.

Finally, put all the letters together to make the code XJTF.

Hints & Tips

Take care and read the question carefully! Make sure you know whether you are being asked to find a code or a word and adapt the technique accordingly.

Always use the alphabet provided. It is there to help you.

Practice Questions

In the following questions some of the words have been written in code. In each question the code has been "broken" for one word. You must use the same code to work out the second word.

A B C D E F G H I J K L M N O P Q R S T U V W X Y Z

Example: If OFYU means NEXT, what does XJME mean? [WILD]

13.1	If VNKE means WOLF, what does MNRD mean?	[ ]
13.2	If PGZV is the code for NEXT, what is the code for POST?	[ ]
13.3	If ABKM means BALL, what does AJQE mean?	[ ]
13.4	If KPMU is the code for FORT, what is the code for JUMP?	[ ]
13.5	If JCOC means RISE, what does KNAN mean?	[ ]
13.6	If DATP is the code for BARN, what is the code for FANG?	[ ]
13.7	If IMXOJ means HOUSE, what does TNRQY mean?	[ ]
13.8	If EUPLH is the code for BROKE, what is the code for PARTY?	[ ]

QUESTION TYPE 14 – "Alphabet Sequences"

Example Question

Using the alphabet shown below identify the next letters in the sequence.

A B C D E F G H I J K L M N O P Q R S T U V W X Y Z

Example: RJ, SH, TF, UD, [VB]

Explanation and Technique

This type of question asks you to identify which letters come next in a given sequence. The best way to explain this is by using the example shown:

Example: RJ, SH, TF, UD,

In these questions letters are presented in pairs, for example, RJ. However, to answer these questions you must identify the sequences associated with the **first and second letter in each pair separately**.

In the example question the first letters in each of the pairs are R, S, T and U. By looking at the alphabet below you will see that the first letter in each pair is **one letter to the right** of the previous one, for example S is one letter to the right of R. Therefore the first letter of the answer will be **one letter to the right** of U in the alphabet, i.e. V. This is shown below:

A B C D E F G H I J K L M N O P Q R S T U V W X Y Z

Now look at the second letters in each pair, J, H, F, and D. Again using the alphabet you can see that each letter is **two letters to the left** of the previous one so the answer will be **two letters to the left** of D, i.e. B.

A B C D E F G H I J K L M N O P Q R S T U V W X Y Z

Although this example question is quite simple other questions may be more complex. However, you still use the same technique. You must identify the sequence of the first letters and then the sequence of the second letters in the pairs. Look at the following sequence. This may appear quite complex at first, but applying the technique will lead you to the answer.

PZ, KY, GX, DW, BV

Starting with the first letters in the pairs, K is 5 letters to the left of P in the alphabet, G is 4 letters to the left of K, D is 3 letters to the left of G and B is two letters to the left of D. The first letter in the answer will therefore be **A** which is one letter to the left of B. This is shown below:

A B C D E F G H I J K L M N O P Q R S T U V W X Y Z

Now look at the second letters in the pairs. Each letter is immediately to the left of the previous one so the answer will be one letter to the left of V, i.e. **U.**

All you need to do now is to put the letters A and U together to arrive at the answer **AU**.

Hints & Tips

Always use the alphabet provided. This will save time and minimize mistakes.

Always treat the first and second letters separately.

Look at the sequence for all the letters. Never try and guess what is likely to happen next in the sequence.

Practice Questions

Using the alphabet shown below identify the next letters in the sequences.

A B C D E F G H I J K L M N O P Q R S T U V W X Y Z

Example: DQ, GO, JM, MK, [PI]

14.1	BR, DS, FT, HU,	[ ]
14.2	JJ, KI, LH, MG,	[ ]
14.3	QA, QF, RK, RP, SU,	[ ]
14.4	JF, IH, HL, GR, FZ,	[ ]
14.5	CE, DG, FI, IK, MM,	[ ]
14.6	KZ, MX, OV, QT, SR,	[ ]
14.7	MM, OK, QI, SG,	[ ]
14.8	IF, JH, HJ, KL, GN,	[ ]

QUESTION TYPE 15 – "Word Combination"

Example Question

In this question find **two** words, one from each group, which make a new word when combined. The word from the group on the left must come first.
Example: [growl, <u>spar</u>, rage]   [<u>row</u>, rush, bond]

Explanation and Technique

For these questions you must put two words together to make a new word. You must use one word from the left-hand brackets and one word from the right-hand brackets but the word in the left-hand brackets must come first. In the example above, adding *spar* to *row* results in the new word *sparrow.*

The best way to answer these questions is to work systematically from left to right.

Start by adding the first word in the left-hand brackets to the first word in the right-hand brackets to see if a new word is formed. If a new word isn't formed then add the first word in the left-hand brackets to the second word in the right-hand brackets and then to the third word in the right-hand brackets.

If a new word isn't formed by adding the first word in the left-hand brackets to the words in the right-hand brackets then go on to the second word in the left-hand brackets. Add this to all the words in the right-hand brackets to see if you find the word. Continue with this technique until you make a new word.

Hints & Tips

Do not waste time - as soon as you have found a new word, move on to the next question.

Work carefully and methodically from left to right.

Practice Questions

In these questions find **two** words, one from each group, which make a new word when combined. The word from the group on the left must come first. ***Example:*** [wild, <u>but</u>, rose] [<u>ton</u>, lead, right]		
15.1	[bold, stamp, wit]	[her, hose, camp]
15.2	[car, rid, stare]	[ruin, go, hand]

15.3	[shop, haste, rich]	[ping, past, glass]
15.4	[head, stale, palm]	[hat, line, dark]
15.5	[rush, speak, par]	[first, delve, ties]
15.6	[fell, cot, help]	[van, deafen, ton]
15.7	[mount, cart, pale]	[wet, ridge, farm]
15.8	[bar, rise, dear]	[king, greedy, post]

QUESTION TYPE 16 – "Start and End"

Example Question

In the question below find a letter that goes at the end of one word and the start of the other. The **same** letter must fit in both sets of brackets.

Example: ben [d] art han [d] ream

Explanation and Technique

To answer these questions you need to find **one** letter that goes in **both sets of brackets** to complete the words outside the brackets.

Start with the left-hand words and try to find a letter that will finish the first word and start the second. If you can't see the letter immediately quickly go through the alphabet until you find a letter that is suitable. Once you have done this see if the letter is appropriate for the second set of words.

If the letter isn't suitable then go back to the first set of words and continue going through the alphabet until you find another letter that works. Then try and see if this is suitable for the second set of words again. Continue this technique until you have found a letter that is suitable for both sets of words.

Hints & Tips

If you are taking a multiple-choice version of the test, use the letters shown on the answer sheet to find the answer. Just insert each of the letters from the answer sheet into the question until you find the answer.

Practice Questions

In the questions below find a letter that goes at the end of one word and the start of the other. The **same** letter must fit in both sets of brackets.

Example: roo [m] ate pal [m] eal

16.1	boo	[ ]	iss	tea	[ ]	oose
16.2	wris	[ ]	ent	gree	[ ]	eal
16.3	wis	[ ]	ole	bas	[ ]	elp
16.4	fai	[ ]	uler	roa	[ ]	ice
16.5	jum	[ ]	ear	gri	[ ]	roud
16.6	do	[ ]	oad	fas	[ ]	ent
16.7	glaz	[ ]	vent	vas	[ ]	asy
16.8	bea	[ ]	oala	wal	[ ]	ick

QUESTION TYPE 17 – "Three Pairs"

Example Question

In the following question there are three pairs of words. The second word in each pair of brackets has been formed in the **same way** by using letters from the first word in the brackets.

Find the word that completes the last pair of words.

Example: [cold old] [bright right] [start tart]

Explanation and Technique

In these questions the second words in each set of brackets has been formed by using letters from the first word in the brackets. In the example above, the second word in the brackets has been formed by removing the first letter of the first word and so, for example, c is removed from the word **c**old to make the word old. This same technique has been used in the second set of brackets where b has been removed from **b**right to form right.

In the last set of brackets the word tart has been formed by removing the first letter of **s**tart.

To answer these questions start by looking at the two words in the first brackets and identify which letters have been used from the first word to make the second word. Once you have identified this then check your assumption by using the words in the second brackets. If your assumption is correct then use the same technique to form the missing word in the third set of brackets.

Hints & Tips

Always work methodically. Start with the words in the first set of brackets.

Remember that the word you are trying to find must be a real word.

Practice Questions

In the following questions there are three pairs of words. The second word in each pair of brackets has been formed in the **same way** by using letters from the first word in the brackets.

Find the word that completes the last pair of words.

Example: [tear tea] [ride rid] [bare bar]

17.1	[dark ark] [brim rim] [fare ?]
17.2	[white hit] [slips lip] [stare ?]
17.3	[party tar] [lunge gun] [beats ?]
17.4	[scrape pea] [appeal ale] [saddle ?]
17.5	[rotten net] [minnow won] [loaned ?]
17.6	[watch hat] [lower row] [butch ?]
17.7	[wasp was] [ride rid] [wart ?]
17.8	[spin nip] [rung gnu] [stop ?]

QUESTION TYPE 18 – "Word Groupings"

Example Question

In the following question find **two** words that are **different** from the others.

Example: [cod, mackerel, haddock, <u>crab</u>, <u>shell</u>]

Explanation and Technique

Here you are given a group of five words. Three of the words are related in some way. You need to try and find the two words in the group that are <u>not related</u> to the others. In the example above all the words are things that are found in the sea but cod, mackerel and haddock are fish whereas crab and shell are not.

Hints & Tips

Do not spend too much time on each question! As soon as you have found the two words go to the next question. It is very easy to spend too much time on this type of question.

Practice Questions

In the following questions find **two** words that are **different** from the others.

Example: [apple, pear, <u>carrot</u>, orange, <u>cabbage</u>]

18.1	[dinghy, yacht, car, wagon, ship]
18.2	[buzzard, sparrow, osprey, eagle, pigeon]
18.3	[lamb, sheep, foal, calf, cow]
18.4	[daffodil, beech, tulip, oak, snowdrop]
18.5	[rugby, football, cycling, running, tennis]
18.6	[Manchester, London, Brussels, Paris, Germany]
18.7	[guitar, harp, trumpet, trombone, violin]
18.8	[gram, kilo, metre, kilometre, pound]

QUESTION TYPE 19 – "Number Relationships"

Example Question

In this question the three numbers in each group are related in exactly the same way. Calculate the number to complete the third group.

Example: (3 [6] 9) (4 [8] 12) (4 [12] 16)

Explanation and Technique

In these questions you are given three sets of numbers contained within brackets. You need to work out how the numbers in the first and second brackets are related and use this same relationship to work out the missing number in the third set of brackets.

Start by studying the first set of brackets to see what relationship exists between the numbers in the brackets. Once you have found a relationship, use the numbers in the second set of brackets to validate your approach before using the same approach to calculate the missing number in the third set of brackets.

In the example above the numbers in the square brackets are calculated by subtracting the first number from the third number in the rounded brackets. For example, in the first set of brackets 6 is calculated by subtracting 3 from 9. The same relationship exists for the second set of brackets. Therefore to calculate the missing number you must subtract 4 from 16 to give the answer of 12.

In some cases you might need to do something in addition to just adding, subtracting, multiplying or dividing the numbers. Look at the following example:

Example: (2 [7] 4) (3 [10] 6) (1 [ ] 5)

In this example, you need to add the first and last numbers in the round brackets and then add one to calculate the number in the square brackets. For example in the first set of brackets, 2 + 4 = 6 so you need to add one to arrive at 7. The same technique applies to the second brackets; 3 + 6 plus 1 equals 10. Therefore to calculate the missing number in the third set of brackets you must add 1 to 5 and then add one to arrive at the answer. In this case, the answer is 7.

Hints & Tips

Work methodically. Start with the first set of brackets and see whether adding, subtracting, multiplying or dividing the other numbers calculates the number in the square brackets.

If the number in the square brackets is smaller than any of the other numbers in the brackets then think about subtracting or dividing the other numbers. If the number in the square brackets is bigger than the other numbers in the group then you will usually need to either add or multiply the numbers.

Practice Questions

In these questions the three numbers in each group are related in exactly the same way. Calculate the number to complete the third group. *Example:* (10 [9] 1) (8 [5] 3) (9 [3] 6)			
19.1	(6 [15] 9)	(5 [9] 4)	(4 [ ] 6)
19.2	(2 [6] 8)	(5 [10] 15)	(11 [ ] 20)
19.3	(3 [18] 6)	(4 [24] 6)	(8 [ ] 4)
19.4	(8 [4] 2)	(20 [2] 10)	(25 [ ] 5)
19.5	(121 [11] 11)	(120 [10] 12)	(36 [ ] 9)
19.6	(16 [32] 2)	(9 [81] 9)	(14 [ ] 3)
19.7	(8 [1] 7)	(12 [7] 5)	(4 [ ] 4)
19.8	(7 [28] 11)	(4 [23] 9)	(21 [ ] 9)

QUESTION TYPE 20 – "Opposites"

Example Question

In the question below find **two** words, one from each group, that are **opposite** in meaning.

Example: [wild, old, white] [tame, pretty, press]

Explanation and Technique

To answer this type of question you need to find **one word from each set of brackets** that mean the opposite.

The best way to approach the questions is to start by looking at the first word in the first set of brackets and compare this to the words in the second brackets. Work systematically from left to right. If you find a word that is opposite in meaning mark your answer on the question paper or answer sheet.

If there isn't a word that is opposite in meaning then look at the second word in the first brackets and, working from left to right, compare this to the words in the second brackets. If you still haven't found a word that is opposite in meaning look at the final word in the first brackets and compare this to all the words in the second set of brackets.

Hints & Tips

Read the question carefully! In some questions you may be asked to find two words that are **most similar** in meaning (for example fast and quick).

Work systematically from left to right - that way you won't miss anything.

Move to the next question as soon as you have found an answer. Do not waste time looking for other alternatives.

Practice Questions

In the questions below find **two** words, one from each group, that are **opposite** in meaning.

Example: [shallow, press, withered] [sordid, solid, deep]

20.1	[love, now, wet]	[dry, jump, risk]
20.2	[nest, safe, quench]	[stare, dangerous, stamp]
20.3	[wrestle, bold, pinch]	[snake, timid, fast]
20.4	[best, tape, huge]	[large, diminish, worst]
20.5	[sprint, wealthy, tidy]	[ugly, poor, groan]
20.6	[rapid, happy, tired]	[brave, helpful, slow]
20.7	[borrow, worry, loud]	[determined, delicate, quiet]
20.8	[angular, fragile, clear]	[wicked, sturdy, kind]

QUESTION TYPE 21 – "More or Less"

Example Question

Jayne, Maria, Richard, Peter and Patricia all play golf.

Maria, Peter and Richard play football and tennis.

Jayne plays volleyball and basketball.

Patricia, Jayne, and Peter play rugby.

Maria and Peter play table tennis.

Work out who plays the **fewest** sports.

Explanation and Technique

In this type of question you are given quite a lot of information and need to put it into an order so that you can analyse it. The best way to answer the example question shown above is to make a table showing the people and the sports they play. An example table is shown below.

	Golf	Football	Tennis	Volleyball	Basketball	Rugby	Table Tennis
Jayne	✓			✓	✓	✓	
Maria	✓	✓	✓				✓
Richard	✓	✓	✓				
Peter	✓	✓	✓			✓	✓
Patricia	✓					✓	

The ticks show the sports that people play. Once the information is put in a table format it is very easy to see that Patricia plays the fewest sports.

Hints & Tips

Always create a rough table – this should take very little time and will avoid you making any errors.

Read the question carefully to make sure you know what is being asked for. In the example above you are asked who plays the **fewest** sports but you could have been asked who plays the **most** sports.

Practice Questions

21.1	Pedro, Dirk, Molly and Asher each own a hamster. Pedro, Molly and Dirk own a cat each. Asher and Sam both have a dog and a ferret. Sam, Molly, and Pedro each keep a goldfish. Molly owns a horse. Who has the fewest pets?

21.2	Florence, Tony and Natasha study Maths, English and Biology. Florence and Tony study Chemistry and French. Natasha studies Art and Drama. Tony and Natasha study Geography. Tony studies Spanish. Who is studying the most subjects?

QUESTION TYPE 22 – "True or False?"

Example Question

Anthony, Vera and Terence need to be able to complete a cross-country course in less than 12 minutes to join the school running team.

Anthony and Vera can both complete the course in less time than Terence.

Terence's fastest time for completing the course is 12 minutes and 23 seconds.

Which one of the following must be true?

A. Terence doesn't join the school running team.

B. None of the runners join the school team.

C. Only Vera joins the running team.

D. Anthony is offered a place in the running team but decides not to accept it.

E. Vera and Anthony join the school running team.

Explanation and Technique

In this type of question you are given some information and must use this to validate the statements that are provided to decide which the best answer is. In the above example we are told that you must be able to run the cross-country course in **less than 12 minutes** to be able to join the school team. We are also told that Terence's best time to complete the course is 12 minutes and 23 seconds. This is **more than** the time needed to get a place in the school team.

Therefore option **A** is the correct one since Terence is not fast enough to join the school running team. The other options **might** be true but you are not given enough information to validate these.

Hints & Tips

Do not make assumptions - only use the information provided in the question.

Practice Questions

22.1	Rodney, Derek and Pierre need to be able to run a marathon in less than 4 hours to get a certificate from their school. Rodney and Pierre can complete the marathon in less than 4 hours. Derek's time for running the marathon is more than Rodney and Pierre. Which one of the following must be true? A. Rodney and Pierre are able to receive certificates. B. Derek, Rodney and Pierre all receive certificates. C. No one receives a certificate. D. Rodney is faster at running the marathon than Pierre. E. Derek can run the marathon in less than 4 hours.

22.2	Alison, Fatima and Louise need £6 each to go bowling. Alison has £5.50. Fatima and Louise both have more money than Alison. Which one of the following must be true? A. Fatima, Alison and Louise all go bowling. B. Alison borrows some money so that she can go bowling. C. Fatima has more money than Louise. D. Louise doesn't go bowling. E. Alison can't go bowling.

QUESTION TYPE 23 – "Time Trial"

Example Question

Rupert, William and Steven catch trains to go to the same destination.

Rupert catches the 11.30 am train.

William's train journey takes half as long as Steven's.

William's train leaves 15 minutes before Rupert and arrives at 12.30 pm.

Steven catches the 11.45 am train.

What time does Steven arrive at the destination?

Explanation and Technique

The best way to answer this type of question is to write down the information provided in an easily understandable format. For the above example, you should create a table like that shown below:

	Depart	**Arrive**	**Journey Time**
Rupert	11.30 am		
William	11.15 am	12.30pm	45 mins
Steven	11.45 am		

Revision

Please note that William's arrival time is 12.00 and not 12.30 as stated in the example question.

We apologise for this error.

Start by filling in the information that you are given and then use this to calculate the other values.

William's departure time is easily calculated since he leaves 15 minutes before Rupert who leaves at 11.30 am.

William's journey time of 45 minutes can be easily calculated since he departs at 11.15am and arrives at 12.30pm. The question tells you that William's journey time is half the time of Steven's journey time so Steven's journey time must be 90 minutes (i.e. 2 x 45 minutes).

To find Steven's arrival time you just need to add 90 minutes to the departure time of 11.45 to get the answer of 1.15 pm.

Hints & Tips

Remember to create a table so that you can present the information in a format that is easy to understand.

Practice Questions

23.1	A12, B17, C19 are the codes for flights from Heathrow Airport to the same destination. A12 leaves at 21.00. B17 takes 1 hour longer than C19. C19 leaves at 17.00 and arrives at 20.00. B17 leaves ten hours before A12. What time does B17 arrive at the destination?

23.2	Esther, Andrew and Sven are all bus drivers who drive from Manchester to London. Esther takes 2 hours longer than Andrew because of traffic jams. Sven leaves at noon and arrives at 5 pm. Andrew leaves 30 minutes before Sven and arrives 1 hour earlier. Esther leaves at 10.00 am. What time does Esther arrive in London?

23.3	W, X and Y are all cars travelling from Glasgow to the same location. W leaves at midnight and arrives at 3 am. X's journey time is 1 hour greater than Y. Y leaves 90 minutes after W and arrives at the same time. X leaves at 4 am. What time does X arrive at the destination?

Answers to Practice Questions

1.1	3	4.1	child entered	7.1	bar
1.2	C	4.2	Water makes	7.2	her
1.3	B	4.3	boys and	7.3	row
1.4	0	4.4	that she	7.4	rat
1.5	12	4.5	computer never	7.5	ant
1.6	C	4.6	When should	7.6	tea
1.7	64	4.7	borrow something	7.7	rot
1.8	C	4.8	the road	7.8	key
2.1	Break	5.1	raise & higher	8.1	4887
2.2	Free	5.2	mobile & movable	8.2	7253
2.3	Well	5.3	rest & relax	8.3	FORCE
2.4	Lie	5.4	pull & drag	8.4	4273
2.5	Trip	5.5	refine & improve	8.5	FARE
2.6	Stick	5.6	jest & joke	8.6	5263
2.7	Beam	5.7	wail & cry	8.7	DEER
2.8	Grave	5.8	smear & spread	8.8	FACE
3.1	England & Italy	6.1	ALL & FEAR	9.1	MF
3.2	hot & last	6.2	HOSE & FOUND	9.2	XM
3.3	knows & right	6.3	ART & CROW	9.3	GK
3.4	rocket & ship	6.4	EACH & REAR	9.4	WU
3.5	ran & walked	6.5	FOR & MOUTH	9.5	ZS
3.6	flower & tree	6.6	SCAR & FARM	9.6	YP
3.7	ancient & high	6.7	OWN & NEWT	9.7	LP
3.8	goose & fish	6.8	OWL & FEEL	9.8	PI

10.1	12	13.1	NOSE	16.1	m
10.2	9	13.2	RQUV	16.2	t
10.3	42	13.3	BIRD	16.3	h
10.4	0	13.4	OVHQ	16.4	r
10.5	1	13.5	STEP	16.5	p
10.6	4	13.6	HAPI	16.6	t
10.7	31	13.7	SPOUT	16.7	e
10.8	2	13.8	SDSUB	16.8	k
11.1	DEAR	14.1	JV	17.1	are
11.2	LATE	14.2	NF	17.2	tar
11.3	DARK	14.3	SZ	17.3	tea
11.4	RICE	14.4	EJ	17.4	led
11.5	TRAM	14.5	RO	17.5	den
11.6	SLAP	14.6	UP	17.6	hut
11.7	POUR	14.7	UE	17.7	war
11.8	PEAR	14.8	LP	17.8	pot
12.1	22	15.1	wit + her = wither	18.1	car & wagon
12.2	64	15.2	car + go = cargo	18.2	sparrow & pigeon
12.3	8	15.3	shop + ping = shopping	18.3	sheep & cow
12.4	1	15.4	head + line = headline	18.4	beech & oak
12.5	12	15.5	par + ties = parties	18.5	cycling & running
12.6	23	15.6	cot + ton = cotton	18.6	Manchester & Germany
12.7	12	15.7	cart + ridge = cartridge	18.7	trumpet & trombone
12.8	14	15.8	bar + king = barking	18.8	metre & kilometre

19.1	10	20.1	wet & dry	21.1	Dirk
19.2	9	20.2	safe & dangerous	21.2	Tony
19.3	32	20.3	bold & timid	22.1	A
19.4	5	20.4	best & worst	22.2	E
19.5	4	20.5	wealthy & poor	23.1	15.00 (3.00 pm)
19.6	42	20.6	rapid & slow	23.2	16.30 (4.30 pm)
19.7	0	20.7	loud & quiet	23.3	06.30 (6.30 am)
19.8	40	20.8	fragile & sturdy		

Creatures of Arabia

MAMMALS

Mike Unwin and Frances LaBonte

This book would not have been possible without the generous support of Dubai Civil Aviation

First published in 2007 by **JERBOA BOOKS**
PO Box No. 333838 Dubai UAE
www.jerboabooks.com

ISBN 978-9948-431-38-1
رقم إذن الطباعة: 292
التاريخ: 4 مارس 2007

Produced by Cambridge Publishing Management Ltd
Designer: Jane Hawkins
Illustrator: Damien Egan

Printed in India

Cover: Arabian leopard
Title page: Nubian ibex

Picture Acknowledgements
(b = bottom c = centre t = top l = left r = right)
The publisher would like to thank the following for supplying the photographs for this book: © The Trustees of the British Museum. All rights reserved, p31b; Damien Egan, Breeding Centre, Sharjah pp13tr, 16t, 18t, 19t, 21c, 22t, 25b, 43t, 44t; Hanne and Jens Eriksen contents, pp3, 5tr, 7t&c, 10 all, 11t, 12b, 18 (background), 31tr&tl, 32 (both), 33b, 34, 35 (both), 37t, 40r, 44b; Frank Lane Picture Agency (FLPA) pp1, 12t, 18b (leopard), 20t, 25t; Carole Harris pp11b, 13tl, 14b; Marijcke Jongbloed pp5tl, 9c, 14t, 16b, 24, 43b; Gloria Kifayeh 6t, 7b, 15; Oxford Scientific (OSF) cover, pp6b, 8 (both), 9t&b, 13b, 17 (both), 19b, 20b, 21t&b, 22b, 23 (both), 26 (both), 27 (both), 28 (both), 29b, 30, 33t, 36 (both), 37b, 38, 40l, 41 (both), 42, 45; Mike Unwin pp29t, 39t.

An at-a-glance guide to the animals' main habitats:

- Sandy deserts
- Rocky areas, mountains and gravel plains
- Plantations, parks, towns and gardens

CONTENTS

INTRODUCTION

Mammals are warm-blooded creatures. Most of them are covered in fur and have four legs. Mice, cats and horses are typical mammals. Nearly all mammals also give birth to their babies live, whereas birds, fish and reptiles usually lay eggs. A few mammals are different, such as dolphins and bats. Instead of having four legs, dolphins have flippers for swimming, and bats have wings for flying. But all mammals feed their babies on milk.

Life is not easy for mammals in Arabia. The environment is harsh. It is formed mostly of mountains, desert and stony plains, where there is little water and few plants. Mammals have to work hard to find enough food and drink. They also have to cope with very hot weather. In the summer, the temperature can reach 50°C, but it can be very cold in the desert at night.

There are more mammals in Arabia than you might think. If you look closely, you can see their footprints in the sand or their droppings beside a mountain path. These mammals have special ways of living in a tough environment. Most have sandy camouflage colours that make them hard to see. Many live in burrows and only come out at night when it is cooler. Some have clever ways of getting water, which means they can survive even when there's no rain for months.

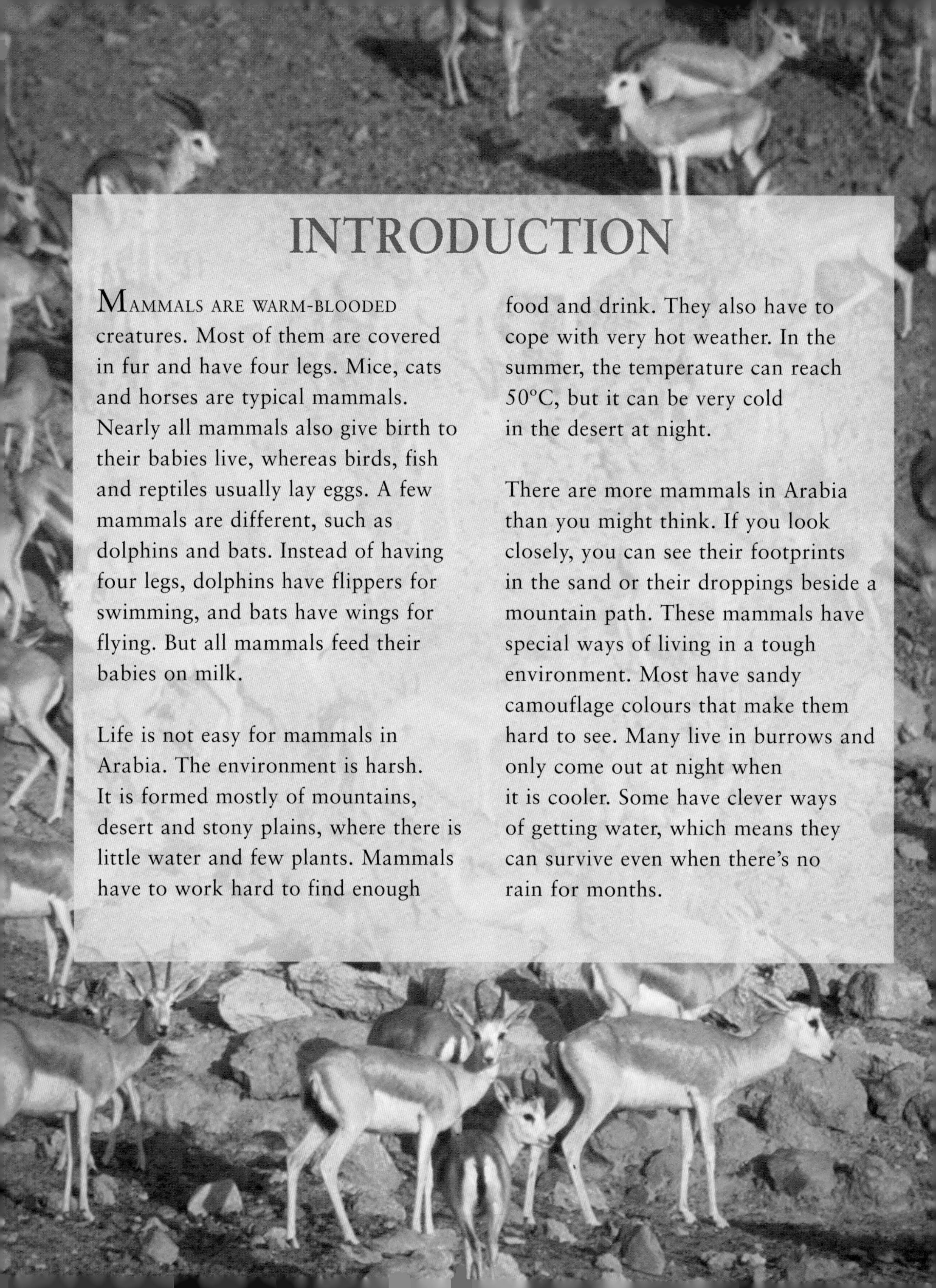

△ This young sand fox has large ears and lives in a burrow. This is typical of desert mammals.

△ The sandy colour of this mountain gazelle helps it blend into its desert background.

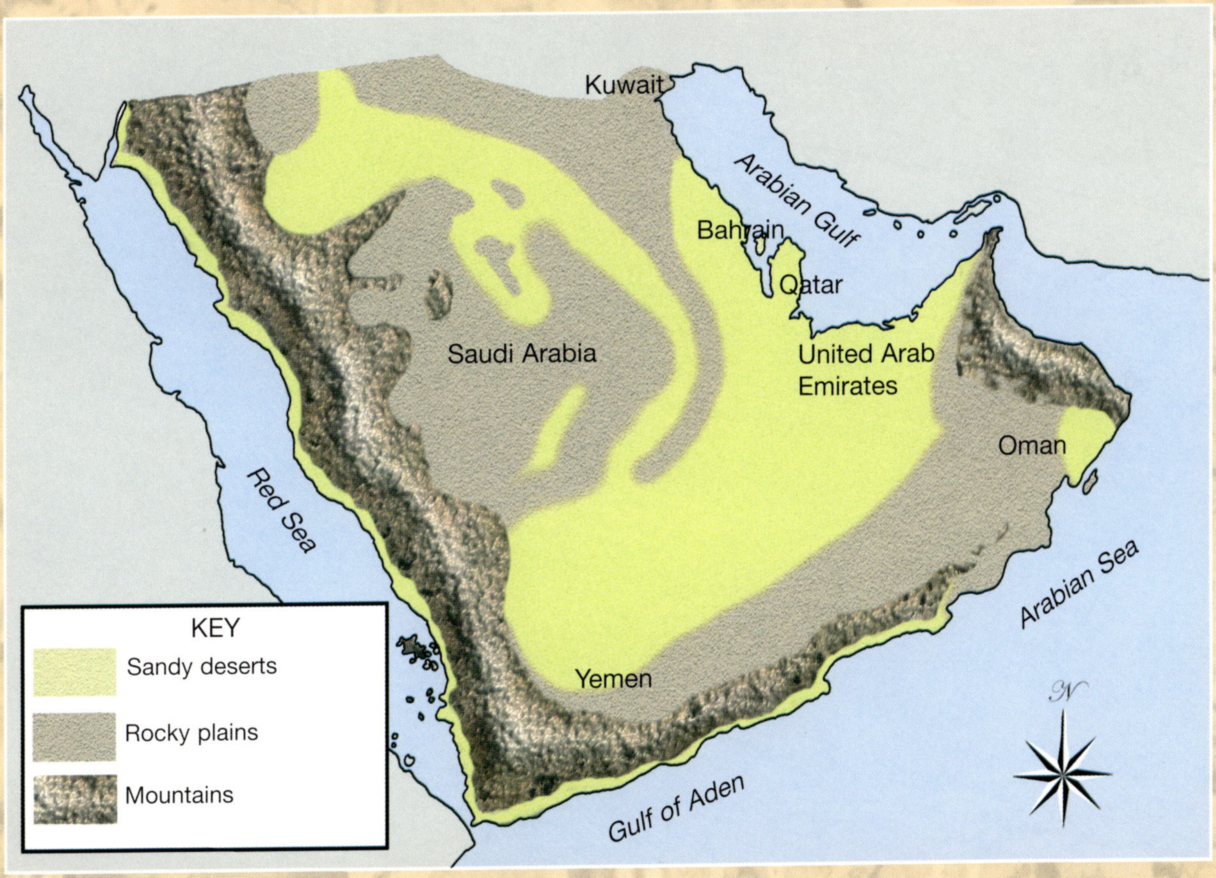

△ This map shows the main natural habitats of Arabia.

ARABIAN CAMELS

THE CAMEL FOUND IN ARABIA is called the dromedary – or one-humped camel. The two-humped (or Bactrian) camel lives in central Asia and has a much thicker coat.

People first domesticated camels in Arabia more than 3,000 years ago. Today, no wild ones are left. For centuries camels have made life easier for desert people by carrying their heavy loads. They do much of their work after dark or early in the morning, and can travel up to 40km per night in long convoys called camel trains. Camels also produce milk, meat, wool and leather. You can even use dried camel dung as fuel. In turn, people have looked after camels, giving them water and food.

◁ A camel mother and her baby. The rope around the mother's front legs is called a hobble. It allows her to wander about, but stops her from running off.

Camels are built to survive desert conditions. They can go without drinking for days. They get moisture from their food, which includes salty plants that other animals avoid. When our body temperature rises we sweat to cool ourselves down. But camels cannot afford to lose moisture, so they get very hot before they start to sweat.

▷ The hump on a camel's back contains fat, not water. But when there's no water to drink, this breaks down inside its body to provide vital energy.

▽ Owners provide water for their camels during very dry spells. Camels can go without drinking for a long time, but then they can swallow more than 100 litres at a go!

▽ A camel can close its nostrils to keep out sand that's blowing around. This also helps it save water, because less moisture evaporates from the lining of its nose.

ARABIAN ORYX

THE ARABIAN ORYX IS A HANDSOME ANTELOPE that is found only in Arabia. Small herds once roamed right across the peninsula. But by 1972 hunters had nearly driven the oryx to extinction in the wild. Luckily, there were still a few in zoos in Europe and America. In 1979, scientists reintroduced some of these to nature reserves in their former desert home. Today hundreds are living wild again.

Oryx are adapted to desert conditions. During summer they feed at night to avoid the daytime heat. Their white coat reflects the sun's rays, so they do not overheat in direct sunshine. Like camels, they can survive for months without drinking. They get the moisture they need from succulent desert plants and dew.

△ A female oryx gives birth to a single calf once a year, usually during winter rains. The youngster's sandy colour helps it to hide from predators.

▽ By day oryx rest in the shade of a tree, or in a shallow pit that they scrape with their horns.

▽ Oryx walk tirelessly to find fresh grass to graze. They follow the smell of recent rain in search of new growth, sometimes covering up to 50km a night. Broad, shovel-shaped hooves help them to cross the soft sand and loose gravel.

▽ The Arabian oryx is the largest Arabian antelope, with males weighing up to 90kg. Its sharp, straight horns can be as long as 90cm. Males use them for fighting and to defend themselves against predators such as leopards or wolves.

DID YOU KNOW?

The oryx's two horns look like just one when seen from side-on. Historians think this might explain how the legend of the unicorn arose.

GAZELLES

GAZELLES ARE SLIM, FAST-RUNNING ANTELOPES that thrive in desert conditions. Two kinds are found in Arabia. Both were common, but are now rare.

Mountain gazelles live in rocky areas and gravel plains, especially where acacia trees grow. Here they wander alone, or in groups of four or six, feeding on small desert shrubs at dawn and dusk, and resting during the heat of the day.

▷ The horns of the male mountain gazelle are thicker than the female's. He uses them to fight and threaten other males in battles over territory.

▽ The mountain gazelle, sometimes called the Arabian gazelle, is smaller than the sand gazelle, weighing just 15–20kg. It has a rich brown coat, with a stripy face and dark stripe along each flank.

▷ A mountain gazelle shares a waterhole with a sandgrouse. It can go without water, but will drink whenever water is available.

▷ Mountain gazelles can escape predators such as wolves by running at speeds of up to 65kph.

The sand gazelle is larger and paler than the mountain gazelle. It is about the size of a goat. It has long, slim horns that are hooked at the tip and a plain coat the colour of the sandy desert where it lives. Its dark eyes, nose and mouth stand out boldly in its face, which becomes white as it grows older.

Sand gazelles live in herds. Just like Arabian oryx, their pale coat helps them to stay cool by reflecting the rays of the sun. A female generally gives birth to twins, which is unusual for antelope. She hides them in a hollow or under a bush until they are ready to join the herd.

▷ Sand gazelles get all the moisture they need from the desert shrubs they eat, and by licking the morning dew off their coats.

IBEX, TAHR AND FERAL GOATS

SEVERAL KINDS OF GOAT LIVE WILD in the mountains of Arabia. These nimble climbers can dash up and down steep slopes, using their rubbery hooves to grip the rocks. They live in small herds, feeding by day and resting by night. During summer they move up high, where it is cooler. In winter they come down to the lower slopes. These days, all wild goats are rare and protected by special laws.

The Nubian ibex has a stocky, sandy-brown body with black and white markings on its legs. Its huge curved horns sweep backwards and can measure more than one metre in length.

▷ Male ibex grow twice as big as females. They hold fierce butting contests to see who will take charge. Those with the biggest horns usually win.

▽ Nubian ibex feed mostly on grass and mountain shrubs.

The Arabian tahr lives mostly in the mountains of Oman. This small goat has reddish-brown hair, short horns and a stripy face. Males have a shaggy coat and small beard.

▷ Female tahr have shorter horns.

◁ Arabian tahr must come down from the mountains every day to find drinking water. They sometimes join gazelles.

▽ Feral goats sometimes reach into trees to nibble fresh leaves.

Domestic goats that have gone wild are called feral goats. Some have long horns and boldly patterned coats. They live all over the plains and mountains of Arabia. Ibex and tahr face stiff competition from domestic and feral goats, which invade their habitats and eat their food. If too many goats graze an area, the plants may never grow back.

DONKEYS AND HORSES

HUNTERS SHOT THE LAST ARABIAN WILD ASS in 1927. The donkeys that roam wild in Arabia today are feral. This means that they come from domesticated, not wild, ancestors.

Domestic donkeys are descended from the African wild ass. They were brought to Arabia to work. Some escaped, while others were set free when they were no longer useful. They soon found a new home in the desert.

◁ Feral donkeys are well adapted to life in deserts, though they need to drink water regularly. Small herds roam widely in search of food.

▽ Donkeys have a stocky build, with short legs, long ears and an upright mane. Their coat is usually greyish, with a dark line along the back and across the shoulders.

DID YOU KNOW?

Feral donkeys cause serious problems for wildlife. When grazing, they rip up the whole plant, leaving nothing for wild animals such as oryx and gazelles.

▷ Arabian horses are smaller and slimmer than European horses, with more arched necks.

Today there are probably no wild horses in Arabia. But horses have a long history here. People first domesticated wild horses in this region about 3,500 years ago, using them to carry soldiers into battle. Today Arabian horses are prized worldwide for their speed, strength and intelligence.

Arabian horses look slightly different to other horses. They have an arched neck and short back, which makes it easier for them to carry a heavy rider. Bedouin stories tell how Allah created the Arabian horse from the four winds. He gave it spirit from the north, strength from the south, speed from the east and intelligence from the west.

DESERT CATS

THE DESERTS OF ARABIA ARE HOME to two small kinds of cat. The wild cat lives in rocky areas and gravel plains. The sand cat lives deep in the sandy desert.

Arabian wild cats are smaller and slimmer than their furry European cousins. They weigh about 3–5kg, and have a greyish-brown coat, orange-brown ears and black rings at the end of their tail. These fierce predators avoid people. They are solitary, hunting at night for small prey such as birds, rodents, snakes and lizards. They don't need to drink. They get moisture from their food.

▷ A wild cat's stripy face looks very similar to a domestic tabby cat's.

▽ A wild cat kitten. Female wild cats have a litter of between one and five kittens. They can fend for themselves at five months old.

DID YOU KNOW?

Wild cats are the ancestors of domestic cats. People first tamed them in Egypt more than 4,000 years ago. Interbreeding with domestic cats is now causing true wild cats to become endangered.

The tiny sand cat, weighing only 2–3kg, is one of the smallest cats in the world. It has creamy-yellow fur, with a few dark stripes and a black-tipped tail. Its furry footpads help protect its feet from the hot sand. They also give it a better grip on the soft, shifting surface.

▷ Sand cats hunt at night for gerbils and other small prey, using their huge ears to detect the slightest movement. By day they shelter in a burrow that they dig for themselves in the sand.

▽ The sand cat is an expert snake catcher. It stuns its victim with a blow to the head, then kills it with a bite to the neck.

LARGER CATS

TWO BIGGER CATS, THE LEOPARD AND THE CARACAL, roam the more remote areas of Arabia. These shy predators are seldom seen. Farmers blame them for killing sheep and goats, so often try to get rid of them.

△ Arabian leopards are smaller than most leopards in Africa and Asia, and have a greyer coat.

The leopard is Arabia's only true 'big cat'. It weighs about 30kg, and has a beautiful spotted coat and a long tail. Arabian leopards are very rare. There are only about 200 left in the wild, living in remote mountain regions where they are specially protected. Leopards feed on anything from small rodents to larger animals such as ibex. They hunt by day or night, using cover to creep up stealthily on their prey.

▽ A leopard's long tail helps it to balance when running or jumping among the rocks.

The caracal is about half the size of a leopard, weighing up to 15kg. It has a reddish-brown coat, tufted ears, long legs and a short tail. This solitary cat is mostly nocturnal, though during cooler weather it may also hunt by day. Its prey ranges from birds such as partridges to animals as big as gazelles.

△ A caracal hunts by sneaking up close to its prey, then springing on it with a powerful leap.

▷ People used to think that caracals wiggled their ear tassels to lure prey closer.

DID YOU KNOW?

People in ancient times prized caracals for their bird-catching skills and trained them for hunting.

FOXES

FOXES ARE WILD MEMBERS OF THE DOG FAMILY. They hunt by night, using their excellent eyesight, smell and hearing. Several species live in Arabia.

The red fox ranges from Europe and Africa to Asia and America. In Arabia it has spread to most areas where people live, including towns. Red foxes feed on small animals, fruits and carrion. They also scavenge from people's rubbish. They can find food almost anywhere, which is why they are so common.

▷ Red foxes are the largest of Arabia's three foxes, weighing up to 5kg. Their coat is a mixture of rusty-red and greyish-brown.

The sand fox, also called Rüppell's fox, lives in dry regions. It is smaller than the red fox – about the size of a small cat. It has shorter legs, bigger ears and a bushier tail.

◁ Rüppell's fox has a pale sandy-coloured coat. A male and female stay together for life.

▷ The sand fox wraps its bushy tail around its nose and paws to keep warm on cold desert nights.

Blanford's fox is even smaller than the sand fox and lives only in rocky areas. This pretty little animal has a thick, soft coat with a variable pattern of grey and brown. It also has black markings on the legs and tail, and around the eyes.

▽ Unlike the sand fox, which has furry pads, Blanford's fox has naked pads on its feet. This helps it to grip when scrambling around rocky cliffs and hillsides.

▷ Huge ears help Blanford's fox to hear small prey such as lizards. They also help it to lose heat from its body in order to cool down.

WOLVES AND JACKALS

THE ARABIAN WOLF AND ASIATIC JACKAL ARE two larger members of the dog family found in Arabia. Today both are endangered in Arabia.

The wolves that live in Arabian deserts belong to the same species that lives in the forests of Europe and North America. But Arabian wolves hunt in pairs or small groups, not in big packs. Their prey ranges from rodents to animals as large as goats. For many years farmers killed wolves, which sometimes took their livestock. Today wolves are protected and their numbers are beginning to increase.

▷ A true Arabian wolf has yellow eyes. Mixed-race wolves have brown eyes.

▽ The Arabian wolf is smaller than its northern cousins, standing about 70cm at the shoulder and weighing 20–30kg. It also has a shorter, beige-coloured coat.

DID YOU KNOW?

Arabian wolves, just like wild cats, are threatened by the spread of their domestic cousins. Wild wolves may interbreed with feral dogs that they meet at desert drinking places. This leaves fewer pure wolves in the wild.

The Asiatic jackal, also called golden jackal, is somewhere between a fox and a wolf in size. Just like a wolf, its long thin legs are built for running after prey. Jackals catch anything from ground birds to young gazelles. They also eat fruit and carrion. Pairs stay together for life. They share the work of hunting and raising their cubs.

▽ Jackals sometimes scavenge along beaches and rubbish dumps, eating anything they can find.

STRIPED HYENAS

THE STRIPED HYENA IS A SECRETIVE NOCTURNAL animal. It is an expert at living on food that others leave behind.

At first glance this medium-sized carnivore looks like a dog. But look closer and you'll see differences. It has a sloping shape, with shoulders higher than its hips. It also has a long neck, a broad muzzle, pointed ears and a short bushy tail. Its yellowish-grey coat is patterned with black stripes.

▽ The long mane along a hyena's spine sticks up when it feels threatened, making it appear bigger to its enemies.

DID YOU KNOW?

Hyenas do an important waste disposal job. They clean up carcasses, which helps to stop diseases from spreading.

Striped hyenas live together in small family groups called clans, but they forage alone. They like open, rocky country, preferably close to water, and sometimes visit beaches to search for food. Today most striped hyenas live in remote parts of Arabia, and they have not been seen in the UAE for many years. But these animals wander great distances and may often go unnoticed.

▷ Striped hyenas use their strong jaws and teeth to scavenge from animal carcasses, even crunching up bones and hooves. They also sometimes hunt weak or injured animals, and will snap up reptiles, insects and fruit. Occasionally they visit rubbish dumps in search of food. They will even raid farms for melons.

▽ Striped hyenas sometimes bask by the entrance to their den in the cool of the evening.

HONEY BADGERS

THE HONEY BADGER IS ONE OF NATURE'S TOUGHEST CUSTOMERS. It can climb trees, dig holes, catch snakes and keep walking all night. It will defend itself so fiercely that even a leopard leaves it alone. Though once widespread across Arabia, honey badgers are now uncommon.

Honey badgers sound so scary that you might expect them to be big. In fact they are only the size of a small dog. The males weigh 10–14kg. They have a compact body with a short tail, and strong legs with long claws.

▷ A honey badger is coloured black below and silvery grey above. Scientists think this striking pattern warns other animals to keep away – just like the yellow and black stripes of a wasp.

▽ Honey badgers need plenty of space. They can wander more than 30km per night in search of food.

△ Honey badgers eat honey – of course! They use their long claws to break into bees' nests. Their thick skin helps protect them from being stung by the angry owners.

A honey badger's tough, loose skin helps it to wriggle free from an enemy's grip. When threatened, it growls and rushes at its attacker. If that fails, it squirts a nasty-smelling spray from its rear end.

▷ Honey badgers also eat carrion, fruit and small animals, and use their strong sense of smell to track down food. They are experts at catching dangerous snakes. They also dig gerbils out of their burrows, blocking up the exit holes so the rodents can't escape.

MONGOOSES

MONGOOSES ARE SMALL, LONG-TAILED CARNIVORES that slink low to the ground on short legs. Four different species live in Arabia: three hunt by day, and one by night.

The Indian grey mongoose is the smaller and more common of the Arabian mongooses, weighing just 1–1.5kg. This small agile predator has brownish-grey fur and normally a dark-tipped tail. It also has a small round head with small ears and a short nose.

△ The Indian grey mongoose likes rocky areas with plenty of nooks and crannies. It can climb trees and walls in search of prey.

Experts think people probably introduced the Indian grey mongoose to Arabia from Iran. Today it lives happily around towns and villages, feeding on rodents and reptiles – including vermin such as rats. It hunts alone and by day.

▽ The Indian grey mongoose is an expert snake catcher. It is not immune to their venom, as some people think, but uses speed to dodge their bites. Once a snake becomes exhausted, the mongoose kills it with a swift bite to the head.

The cat-sized white-tailed mongoose is twice as big as the Indian grey. It has longer legs and a more fox-like face. It is also harder to see, since it lives in mountainous areas and only comes out at night. Despite its larger size, this mongoose feeds mostly on insects. It forages alone, nose to the ground, as it searches for food and digs up juicy titbits with its long claws.

▽ You can tell a white-tailed mongoose by its pointed face, black legs and bushy tail – which is usually mostly white.

SACRED BABOONS

SACRED BABOONS, ALSO CALLED HAMADRYAS BABOONS, are the only monkeys found in Arabia. They live in rocky and mountainous areas, sometimes close to coastal towns, where they can cause problems by raiding farms and villages for food.

Like all baboons, they are intelligent and sociable animals that live together in groups, called troops. One troop usually contains 50 to 100 members. The adult males are in charge. They protect the others, decide where to go each day and punish any younger baboons that misbehave.

Baboons forage by day. They are omnivorous, eating everything from roots and bulbs to insects and even hares. They also dig in the sand to find water. Males are much larger than females. They weigh up to 30kg, and have a thick cape and ruff of silver-grey fur around their shoulders. Females and young have shorter muzzles (jaws and nose) than adult males, and shorter, browner fur.

▽ Baboons communicate using both their voices and their faces. Baring their sharp teeth while flashing their pale eyelids is a threat. Grinning with eyelids lowered means they are afraid. A loud bark is an alarm call, while gentle muttering is a greeting.

▷ At night baboons move to a cliff ledge, where they are safe from enemies such as leopards.

▽ Youngsters ride on their mother's back. They cling on tightly as she clambers over the rocks.

DID YOU KNOW?

These animals are called sacred baboons because the ancient Egyptians worshipped them. Hamadryas, the baboon god, was thought to stand for Thoth, the god of writing. Baboons were often buried in the tombs of important people.

◁ The ancient Egyptians made many carvings of baboons.

ROCK HYRAXES

THE ROCK HYRAX LOOKS A LITTLE LIKE A LARGE GUINEA PIG, with its furry body, short legs, tiny ears and stumpy tail. But it is not a rodent at all. It belongs to an order of animals whose ancestors were more closely related to elephants.

Look out for hyraxes in rocky areas in western Arabia. They live together in small colonies among boulders. You can often spot a colony from the yellowish-white patterns left by their urine on the cliffs below. Hyraxes are expert at clambering over the rocks, and dash straight up a cliff or disappear into a crack in the rocks at the first sign of danger.

While a group of hyraxes is feeding, a few members of the colony keep a lookout for danger. Their enemies include predators such as caracals and eagles.

▷ A hyrax's feet have soft rubbery pads that produce sticky sweat. This helps it to grip the rocks as it walks and runs. Long sensitive hairs, called guard hairs, also help it to feel its way through narrow cracks in the rocks.

▽ Hyraxes eat a variety of plants. They graze on grass and sometimes climb trees to nibble leaves.

△ Hyraxes cannot control their body temperature as well as most mammals. At night they huddle together in their dens for warmth. Then, first thing in the morning, they come out to lie on a warm rock and sunbathe.

DID YOU KNOW?

In prehistoric times there were many species of hyrax. Today there are only a few, all of which live in Africa and Arabia.

ARABIAN HARES

◁ Hares often sit perfectly still and rely on their camouflage to escape detection by predators.

The Arabian hare is smaller than its African cousin, the Cape hare. This means it can keep cool more easily and needs less food. Hares like areas with plenty of vegetation to nibble, but can also survive in the desert. People once hunted them with falcons, but this sport is now banned. Now hares are protected, so nobody is allowed to hunt them.

Hares are nocturnal. By day they rest in the shade, often in a hollow or under a bush. At night, when it is cooler, they venture out to feed on grasses and shrubs, from which they get all the moisture they need.

A female gives birth to a litter of between two and four babies, called leverets, in a shallow scrape (nest) called a form. The babies are born fully furred and with their eyes open – unlike baby rabbits, which are born blind and naked in a burrow underground. They can feed themselves after about seven days.

◁ A hare's enormous ears give it exceptionally good hearing, so it can listen out for danger. They also help it to stay cool during the day. Heat escapes from the hare's ears when it gets too hot.

DID YOU KNOW?

A hare often eats its own droppings in order to extract even more moisture from its food. This may sound unpleasant, but it makes good sense for desert survival.

▽ If spotted by a predator, a hare leaps up and dashes off in a zig-zag pattern. Its strong back legs can power it along at over 70km per hour.

GERBILS, JIRDS AND JERBOAS

ARABIA IS HOME TO MANY SPECIES OF RODENT. These little creatures generally live in burrows by day, then come out at night to forage for seeds and other food. Gerbils, jirds and jerboas are rodents that are adapted for life in the desert.

Gerbils have long furry tails and big eyes that help them see in the dark. The ones that people keep as pets come from central Asia, but several species also live in Arabia. Their predators include cats, owls and snakes.

△ Cheesman's gerbil is one of the commonest species. Its soft, yellowish fur matches the sandy desert where it lives.

◁ Gerbils dig elaborate burrow systems with many entrances and passageways. The deepest part is the nest chamber, where they sleep and have their babies.

Jirds are bigger than gerbils. They look more like hamsters, but with a longer, furry tail. Most species are very sociable. They dig their burrows in rocky hillsides.

▷ The king jird is the largest of its kind. It lives in rocky areas in south-western Arabia, at a height of up to 2,200 metres.

▽ The lesser jerboa lives in sandy regions. It has just three toes on each of its long back feet. Tufts of hair on the soles help support it and protect the feet from the hot sand.

Jerboas have huge back feet and a long tufted tail. They hop along on their back legs like tiny kangaroos. They can leap more than one metre to escape from danger. Their long tail helps them balance when jumping. It also supports them when standing still. Jerboas live deep in the desert, where they get enough moisture from their food to survive.

INDIAN PORCUPINES

The Indian porcupine is difficult to see. It is strictly nocturnal and even avoids moonlit nights. But if you are lucky enough to spot one, you will not mistake it for anything else.

Porcupines are rodents, just like mice and gerbils. Like all rodents, they have strong incisor teeth for nibbling their plant food. But otherwise they look nothing like mice or gerbils. Weighing 12–16kg, a porcupine is as big as a small dog and is covered with long black and white spines.

▷ A porcupine's spines are specially toughened hairs that grow in rows along its back. The longest ones grow up to 40cm. The hollow ones on the tail are called quills. When a porcupine meets an enemy, it sticks out its spines to make itself look bigger and rattles the quills as a warning. If the enemy comes too close, the porcupine backs into it. Spines may stick in the animal, causing injuries and infections. Even leopards have died from wounds caused by porcupines.

Porcupines live in a variety of habitats, from rocky hillsides to scrubby plains, but always make their home in burrows. A male and female stick together for life and use the same burrow for many years. They share the work of looking after the babies, which stay inside the burrow for their first nine weeks.

DID YOU KNOW?

Porcupines are fond of gnawing on bones, which you can often spot near the entrance to their burrows. This strengthens their teeth and provides calcium to help their quills grow.

◁ Porcupines have a large nose and a very good sense of smell. This helps them to find roots and bulbs beneath the ground. They forage over a huge area in search of food.

HEDGEHOGS AND SHREWS

HEDGEHOGS AND SHREWS BELONG TO A GROUP OF SMALL ANIMALS called insectivores. This means that they eat mostly insects, not plants like rodents do.

Hedgehogs have a round body covered in sharp spines, which help protect them from predators. They are solitary and nocturnal, emerging at dusk to forage for food. When it gets cold during winter, hedgehogs curl up in their burrow. Their breathing and heartbeat slow down, so they do not have to use up energy to keep warm.

▽ The long-eared hedgehog is the smallest of the Arabian species and has long, pointed ears. It often lives around towns and farmland, where it uses its keen nose to sniff out insects and snails.

△ The Ethiopian hedgehog is slightly larger, with more rounded ears and a dark face. It lives in the desert, usually around wadis and oases.

Brandt's hedgehog lives in the mountains. This is the largest and darkest species, and eats large insects and small reptiles. It can even tackle a snake, grabbing the body in its mouth and trusting its spines to protect it from bites.

Shrews are energetic little creatures with long, twitchy snouts. Their small eyes cannot see very well, so they use touch and smell to find their food – sometimes bumping into things in their path. One common species found in Arabia is the house shrew. It often enters houses, where it helps get rid of insect pests. Another is Savi's pygmy shrew. This tiny animal eats more than its own bodyweight in insects every day, just to stay alive.

▽ Savi's pygmy shrew is the smallest mammal in Arabia. It weighs just two grams – the same as two paperclips.

BATS

BATS LIVE IN CAVES OR OLD BUILDINGS BY DAY and come out to feed at night. They have many special talents, including being the only mammals in the world that can truly fly. Most bats in Arabia are found in farmland and coastal areas.

Some bats eat fruit, while others eat insects. Fruit-eating bats are bigger, with large eyes and fox-like faces. Insect-eating bats have smaller eyes and bigger ears.

▷ Many hundreds of fruit bats, all hanging upside down, live together in a colony.

The Egyptian fruit bat is about the size of a crow, with a wingspan of 60cm. It often feeds around gardens and orchards, looking for fruit such as figs and dates. Sometimes it migrates long distances in search of ripe fruit.

▷ Like those of all bats, the wings of the Egyptian fruit bat are really its front legs with skin stretched between the long fingers.

Insect-eating bats cannot see very well. But their big ears help them to get around and find food by using a special technique called echolocation. The bats make high-pitched noises as they fly, too high for us to hear. These bounce off objects around them to reveal what their surroundings look like and which way their tiny prey is flying.

DID YOU KNOW?

Scientists have calculated that one insect-eating bat can catch more than 600 insects in an hour. Just think how many mosquitoes and other harmful pests bats help us to get rid of!

▽ This mouse-tailed bat is one of at least 25 species of insect-eating bat found in Arabia. It has a bare tail, like a mouse's.

LOOKING AFTER ARABIA'S MAMMALS

WILD MAMMALS IN ARABIA FACE MANY THREATS – especially from people. Some species have already died out. Others are very rare and their future is uncertain. But there are many things we can do to help.

When a species of animal has died out in the wild, we say that it has become 'extinct'. Several mammals, such as the Syrian wild ass, became extinct in Arabia during the 20th century. They could not escape the guns and vehicles of hunters.

▷ Scientists think that the cheetah is now extinct in Arabia. The last wild sighting of this fast-running cat was in Yemen in 1994.

People are taking over places where wild animals once lived undisturbed. Cities and farmed areas have replaced their natural habitats. Pollution, fences and roads make their life more difficult and dangerous. Domestic animals such as goats and donkeys use up their food and damage the environment.

◁ Our rubbish can be harmful to wildlife. Hedgehogs, for instance, can be trapped or hurt by litter.

There is some good news, though. Today, more people in Arabia are becoming concerned about wildlife and taking action to protect it. Governments have passed laws to stop rare species being hunted. They have also created nature reserves and other protected areas where wildlife can live safely. Rare animals, such as Arabian oryx, can now go back to their old homes.

▷ This man is guarding rare Arabian tahr in Oman's Wadi Sareen nature reserve.

FIND OUT MORE

There are many places where you can learn more about Arabia's mammals and how to help protect them. Here are a few:

Books and websites

Wild about cats: Life with Arabia's endangered felines (Marycke Jongbloed, published Barkers Trident Communications, London, 1998)
This book is full of interesting information about Arabia's wild cats. It also tells how the author has helped to rear them and protect them in the wild.

http://uaeinteract.com/nature
This website has lots of useful news and information about mammals and other wildlife in the region.

Conservation organisations

Arabian Oryx Project
This project was established in Oman in 1979 to help the conservation of the Arabian oryx. It now also supports projects to protect other wildlife, including Arabian leopards and Arabian tahr. Find out more at http://www.oryxoman.com

WWF (World Wide Fund for Nature)
This is a worldwide conservation organisation that has a regional base in the United Arab Emirates. Find out about its work in Arabia at:
www.panda.org/about_wwf/where_we_work/asia_pacific/where/united_arab_emirates/index.cfm

GLOSSARY

adaptation feature that helps an animal live in its habitat

ancestors animals that lived in the past that a modern animal has developed from

calcium mineral that helps build bones and teeth

carcass body of a dead animal

carnivore animal that eats mostly meat

carrion meat from animals that have already died

domesticated tamed to live with humans or work for them

endangered very rare; in danger of dying out

evaporate turn to vapour when heated

feral originally domesticated, but now living wild

forage search for food

habitat an animal's natural home, such as a forest or desert

incisor kind of tooth at the front of a mammal's mouth

insectivore animal that eats mostly insects

interbreeding when one kind of animal breeds with another, producing young that are a mixture of the two

migrate make a long, seasonal journey in order to find food

nocturnal active mainly at night

oases places with water and lots of vegetation in the middle of a desert

omnivore animal that eats many things, including both plants and meat

predator animal that hunts other animals for food

reintroduce return animals to a place where they once lived before

rodent type of small mammal, such as a mouse, with sharp incisor teeth for eating plants

scavenge find food from leftovers, such as rubbish tips or dead animals

sociable lives in the company of others

solitary living alone

succulent juicy, full of moisture

supernatural magical, not natural

territory place that an animal defends for breeding or feeding

vermin unwanted, troublesome animal

wadi valley or bed of a stream in the desert that is dry except after rain

warm-blooded having a warm blood temperature that does not change if the temperature around changes

INDEX